# Ireland: You Can't Miss it!

## Terri Karsten

WAGONBRIDGE PUBLISHING

2022

*For Michael & Keevan –*
*May the road rise to*
*meet you!*
*Terri Karsten*
*July 2022*

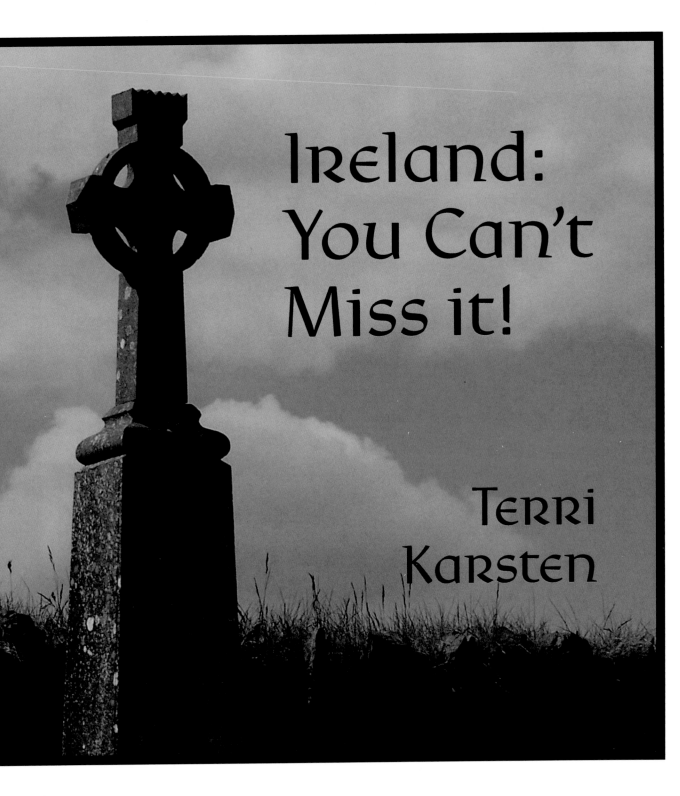

# Ireland: You Can't Miss it!

## Terri Karsten

Wagonbridge Publishing
661 East Howard St.
Winona, MN 55987

First Edition, paperback
ISBN: 978-1-953444-04-2

# Table of Contents

# Getting There and Getting Around

There are many reasons to go to Ireland. It's a place where every corner is steeped in history, and there's always a bit of castle or dolmen or keep on every other field. It's a place where a soft day means light rain, and Leprechauns play shadow tag with the clouds, a place where the little people really could be found and fairy circles abound. Maybe all the snakes have been driven out, but the magic remains.

Ireland is a place where mountains hide sleeping heroes, and hills roll up to the sky and beyond. Ancient stone walls crisscross fields and pastures and roads become rounded tunnels of green, suggesting mystery around the bend. In Ireland, neighbors will watch to see if the old man's car is in and walk up the lane just to see if he's getting on okay. Ireland is a place where my relatives and their friends always ask me how long I'll be home whenever I visit, though I've never lived there at all. Ireland is a place of great beauty with legendary green hills and fields giving reason to the nickname of Emerald Isle. Most of all, Ireland is where my great-grandfather was born and a place my Dad called home. If I needed an excuse, that is reason enough for me to visit many times.

Left: Lane near Stonetown, County Louth
Top: Row houses in Carrickmacross
Right: The cottage, now a shed, where my great-grandather was born

7

The first step in any trip is packing. It ought to be easy, but sometimes doesn't work that way. Inevitably, some needed things are left behind, and some unnecessary items are brought. On one emergency trip to Ireland, I packed in fifteen minutes and remembered everything except socks. Fortunately, I could borrow my dad's until I could buy replacement socks.

Everyone advises packing light. My sisters and I have different ideas about how to pack light. Lisa hates to check a bag because she has lost luggage in the past. I prefer to check a bag because I find it difficult to fit a large carry-on in the overhead compartment on a plane. The real key to packing light is to make sure you can manage all of your own luggage, even on stairs. If you plan on driving, you'll also want to make sure your whole party, along with everyone's luggage, will fit into your rental car, preferably without anyone required to hold a suitcase in their lap. Roads and cars tend to be smaller in Ireland than in the United States, although this is not always true.

Though they do have perfectly good shops and markets in all parts of Ireland, you probably don't want to spend your trip shopping for necessities. Probably the most important thing to bring is a light jacket or sweater and a fold up umbrella since it rains frequently, and can be chilly at any time of the year. Plan to mix and match clothes, and wear most things more than once. It's easy enough to wash a few things, but don't expect anything to dry overnight. On one summer trip, our jeans were still not dry after three days on the line.

There are many ways to get around in Ireland. My first trip there in 1975 as a poor college student involved an overnight ferry to Dublin from Wales, several buses, a bit of hitchhiking, and a lot of walking. Today, both the bus and the train systems of Ireland are quite good. However, if you want to travel on your own schedule or visit smaller, out of the way places, your best bet will be to rent a car.

It used to be nearly impossible to rent an automatic automobile in Ireland. Everyone drove a stickshift. Added to that, remember that cars drive on the left side of the road, and so the driver sits on the right. Even for those of us who can actually drive a stickshift, shifting with the left hand takes some getting used to. Driving on the opposite side of the road also raises other problems for American drivers.

Left turns are much easier, but to make a right turn, you have to remember to go into the far lane, and look the opposite way. Figuring out where your car is in relation to the side of the road is also tricky, especially for those of us with depth perception issues. My sisters and I found it useful to have the front seat navagator say in as calm a voice as possible while gripping the door handle and cringing toward the center of the car, "I think you better move over. You're getting too close to the edge."

Although roundabouts are becoming more common in the United States, the Irish version is also worth mentioning. The theory of the roundabout is that traffic

A view from the plane near Dublin

8

slows, but doesn't stop, so it is more efficient than either a stoplight or a 4-way stop sign for the traffic flow. When everyone knows how to navigate a roundabout, this theory works very well. My problem with this plan is that going into an Irish roundabout I would get a brief glimpse of a complicated sign showing where each of the spokes goes. I had to decipher and memorize which spoke I wanted to take, based not on a road number or name, but on a destination, which may be before or after my intended destination. I generally don't see that fast. One time my husband and I entered a roundabout in a little town near the Burren. We wanted to go straight through, but couldn't tell which spoke led to our route. We went round three times before he decided to follow a truck as the best chance of hitting the right way. The truck took off on what seemed to be an alley, but sure enough a block later it clearly was the main road again.

Irish roads rarely have shoulders and are much narrower than I'm used to. Not taking that into consideration can have drastic consequences. One soft morning we took off after breakfast, heading for the Proleek Dolmen at Ballymascanlon Hotel. As we neared the Hotel, we drifted too far left. It looked like a grassy verge, but was actually a shallow ditch filled with incredibly sharp boulders. Bouncing jarring clunks let us know we had a problem. We pulled into the hotel parking lot and examined the tires. It was bad. The rocks had slashed both passenger side tires. Fortunately, the Irish are wonderfully kind people, and the clerk at the hotel desk helped us ring a garage to come and change the tires for us. Of course, while the car was fixed, we sat for a cup or two of tea. What better way to calm our nerves?

At times it can be difficult to tell a main road from a lane or driveway. Left: R178 and the lane into Dad's cottage, known as Rosslough Lane locally.
Right: L4620, near where it connects back to RI78 at Essexford. R178 is the Carrick Road if you are going west or the Dundalk road heading east.

Not all Irish roads are narrow, one lane tracks, bordered with deep, stony ditches, and thick, hubcap-grabbing hedges, but few of them are actually straight. Whether one lane or more in town or country, the winding roads beckon the traveller on, if just to see what might lie beyond the next bend.

Top left: A side street in Carrickmacross

Bottom left: The local road 4620, near Rosslough, heading toward Coolderry

Top Right: A thru-road in Dundalk

Bottom Right: The backroad lane connecting R178 to L4630

# Getting Lost
# OR
# "You can't get there from here."

**N**either I nor my sisters are blessed with a keen sense of direction, but I would say getting lost in Ireland is easier than just about any place else I've been. In some ways a journal of my last trip to Ireland could be a catalog of where we got lost.

Over the years, I have traveled around Ireland in several different ways, including a disastrous attempt at hitchhiking back in 1975. I say disastrous not because anything bad happened, but only because my two friends and I spent far more time alongside a road lined with blackberry bushes than we did inside a car. When we finally got a ride, from the first car that came by, we went to the nearest town and took a bus for the rest of the trip. Much has changed since 1975. The Irish roads are better, and there are a lot more cars on them. But one thing unchanged is navigating those roads. The Irish have a far different sense of direction than I do. To the Irish, "the top of the town" or "the bottom of road," "just over the hill," and "straight on" all mean something clear and specific, and in the last case, much different from my understanding of the word straight.

Left: The intersection in Slane. Only one way leads to Newgrange, but it's not the way you think. Top: Cars parked illegally in front of the old Toll House in Carrickmacross, where market fees were collected in the nineteenth century. Bottom Right: A sign in Irish and English showing the way to Lisdoonan, which is a bit past Lisnagunnion, where my relatives live.

Above: Kelly's Pub, a well-known if not well marked landmark.

When my sisters and I went to Ireland in 2010, we got lost only once on the way to Dad's cottage in Rosslough. The trouble came in Dundalk. The map seemed to indicate that M1, the road we'd taken out of Dublin, led to Dad's road, R178, but it doesn't. As they say in Ireland, you can't get there from here. You have to take M1 to N52, then to R 178. When we realized we were still going north out of Dundalk, clearly having missed the road we wanted, we stopped at a petrol station to ask directions. I've found the key to getting around in Ireland is a complete willingness to stop and ask directions. Fortunately, everyone we met in Ireland was eager to help us find the way, along with a great deal of advice on how to navigate. The young woman at the counter was no exception.

After greeting her, I said, "We're trying to find R178. Can you help us?"

"Och, we don't know anything about those numbers," she said cheerfully. "We don't use them a'tall. Can ye just tell me where you're going?"

I seriously doubted she knew where my dad lived, as his address has no lane or road number, just a township. But I gave it a try, and said, "We're trying to get to my dad's house. He lives in Rosslough, near Carrickmacross.

"Brilliant." She gave me a warm smile. "Then it's the Carrickmacross road you want. I can tell you that. You take that road and ask around there when you get closer. So go on right here." She gestured to the road in front of the petrol station. "At the lights, turn right again. Go to the bottom of the road and you're right on your way."

I thank her before she could say, "You can't miss it," which seems to be the conclusion of any set of directions in Ireland. The words are meant to reassure the lost wanderer, but they are patently untrue. It is always easy to miss whichever road you've been directed to take.

In this case, her directions worked quite well to get us onto the right road, though I did want to know: how do you tell what is the bottom of the road on a totally level road?

Our directions to Dad's house were rather vague. We were supposed to stay on R178 about 3 or 4 miles past Cluskey's Bar and Restaurant, then turn right into his lane. His was the third or fourth house on that unmarked lane. If we came as far as Kelly's Pub we would have gone too far. We never saw Cluskey's but we did find Kelly's Pub. It's a good thing we'd been there before, because there is no sign or any indication it's a business. The unmarked cottage looks like a yellow-brown house in the middle of the crossroads. As far as I know, the place has not been open on any sort of regular basis for over ten years, though I guess some of the local farmers still frequent it on occasion. It's easy enough to turn around at Kelly's Pub. Retracing our route, we soon saw the large, grey house that serves as the landmark for Dad's lane coming from this direction. Finding your way in Ireland is all about knowing the landmarks.

Apparently, Kelly's Pub is a well-known landmark for miles around. One time we got lost on the unmarked lanes near Tallanstown, which is about six miles from Dad's house in Rosslough. We stopped and asked a gentleman way out in the country to give us directions. He'd never heard of Rosslough, but could give us directions to Kelly's Pub.

As I've said, the Irish are very helpful about giving copious directions and advice, but sometimes a bit gets lost in the translation. Take for instance my cousin Mary's directions to her house.

"From Carrickmacross, go down to the bottom of the town and out past the Shirley Arms, past the petrol store. Don't take the 1st one left. You know Bose? The road down into there, past all the houses and around on in, well don't take that one. Take the 2nd left." She paused, then added, "Don't pay attention to any gravel lanes."

Assuming we could find the right road, we still needed to find her house. There are no house numbers. Mary's house is distinctive because it has a "palm tree hedge". The first time I went there, I was looking for palm trees. There is a house a few doors past Mary's with typical, tall palms. Mary's 'palms,' however, are called cedars in our part of the world.

Some people today have come to rely on GPS or satellite navigation to avoid getting lost. I can tell you from experience that any such reliance is misplaced. We had been in Ireland for several days when we went to visit some cousins and shared our difficulty in finding Newgrange (Brú na Bóinne).

One of the cousins remarked in his delightful Irish accent that he was surprised such a new car didn't have 'set nev'. I let the comment wash over me, since I had no idea what he meant. About 30 minutes later, it dawned on me that 'set nev' probably meant satellite navigation, and I had indeed seen a button on the space-age dashboard that said 'sat'. We all trooped out to the car, and sure enough it did have the program. We got a quick course in how to use it, and all our troubles seemed to be over. Not so. We tried again to go to Brú na Bóinne, since we had not reached it in time to go in on our first trip there. Following Sat Nav, and her lovely, calm, British accent, we arrived at the same stop sign in Slane that we knew so well. Sat Nav insisted we go left, but we knew from long experience that was wrong. That way led only to the kindly gentleman who said, "You can't get there from here."

Above: The old forge at Essexford, across from Kelly's Pub.

# Signs

**G**etting lost in Ireland is not due to a lack of signs. The Irish are just as sign-happy as the rest of the world. In fact, sometimes the confusion comes from too many signs.

Part of the problem for me is where to look for the signs. I'm not used to looking for a street sign on the side of a building, and labeling all the exits of the roundabout in a sign before entering the roundabout requires more memory than I can handle. So if you are driving into Carrickmacross and want the town center, not the outskirts, enter the roundabout, but don't take the exit labeled 'Carrickmacross'. Take the one labled 'Crossmaglen'. I have no idea why this is so, but it's the only way that works.

Left: A sign post in Carlingford
Top: These signs are found leaving Brú na Bóinne. The yellow sign reminds foreigners to drive on the left in three languages, English, French, and German.
Right: The road signs leaving Dublin Airport

Many times the signs in Ireland are not as clear to me as they must be to the Irish. Take crossing signs for an example. Some are delightful, explicit and understandable, like a typical school crossing sign. And if it's important to watch out for young children, it seems reasonable that the elderly might need a crossing sign too. So why not a sign for these unidentified crossers also?

Reading the road often posed a problem for me. As we approached a town, we would see 'SLOW' written in large letters on the road. A bit later, as I was wondering how slow I was meant to go, 'SLOWER' appears, as if the road is screaming at us. Perhaps Irish engineers know drivers never slow down enough. As a side note, gauging how fast to go on any road requires mental math, since speed limits are posted as kilometers per hour. Sometimes we were warned the road ahead had no linings. Other times such road linings as those seen above confused us. I never did figure out if Irish road painters don't know how to do 'straight', or if they just have a zigzag sense of humor.

Warning signs are always helpful to tourists. In Ireland, as anywhere else in the world tourists need help staying safe. It pays to watch out for men working, rocks falling, and stray golf balls

WARNING
BE AWARE OF
GOLF BALLS

Above: Warnings about high waves, schemes for calming unruly traffic, and roads behaving unexpectedly also help the confused tourist to navigate.

Left: A sample roundabout sign tells the driver what to expect.

Roundabout and yield signs both take a minute or so for the foreign driver to process, but this road sign (bottom left) for a construction zone is perfectly clear. And this warning sign (bottom right) leaves no doubt about the dangers ahead.

The three signs on this page, although from various different areas in Ireland, seem to go together, almost like a short story.

"A Stolen Ringbuoy - A Stolen Life"

25

One of the delights of traveling to Ireland comes from the delightful differences in the way we use language. As a side note, I have no idea why this door is marked as a place for wombles, the furry, pointy-nosed creatures first seen in Elizabeth Beresford's children's books in the late 60's. They are known for their propensity to pick up litter and recycle it.

Of course, no matter how clear the sign is in any country, there's always someone who ignores it altogether.

# We all speak English, right?

Ireland and the United States are not exactly two countries divided by a common language, but the differing accents and terms can lead to a rare bit of confusion. Consider the following: My cousin Maura directed me to the top of the town to organize a jam cake for my dad's 80th birthday while she sorted ringing the family. The party started at half eight, but we all had a good 'craic' before eating. Dad drank whiskey while the children had lemonade. I heard their mammies giving out when they spilled some of the fizzy drink. The trouble was sorted with biscuits all around. I was confused when Fergal offered me a wee mineral, but he was just having me on. In the end, everyone agreed t'was a brilliant party.

Confused? So was I, starting with what time to arrive at the party. I discovered that half eight is 8:30 in Minnesota jargon. In the United States we give the kids cookies and soda, and moms scold them when they spill it. Jam cakes are sponge cakes with jam between the layers. While they may need ordering, they never require organizing. In America, we work things out more than we sort them. I drink 7-up, not mineral, and understand the

Left: Dad and my sisters, Lisa, Denise, and Chris, by McNally's, one of Dad's favorite pubs in Carrickmacross.
Top: A shop in Carrickmacross like an old-fashioned five and dime.
Right: I'm sure this is a placement oversight, not a language difference.

jokes when someone is 'having me on.' In Ireland, calling means visiting, and ringing means telephoning, and either one means time for a great 'craic' (That's a chat or shooting the breeze in America). But we can all agree--it was a brilliant party.

Other language differences can take me by surprise too. Gas is petrol and take-out food is called take-away. I never could figure out how to tell the top of the town from the bottom when the town is flat or there are hills in both directions. Nor could I tell how to go straight through in a roundabout.

Most of the time, the American visitor will have no trouble understanding, even if the terms are unfamiliar. For instance, consider the sign to the right. Although we might use a different word for candy, we can appreciate a store with the sense to offer a checkout line that doesn't tempt the tots into whining for a treat.

Left: I'd never heard the term 'dog fouling', but I have no doubt about the meaning here.
Right: There's no confusion about this sign at Brú na Bóinne either, but for those of us who grew up in the 60's and 70's, it offers a good laugh. Pictured: Lisa and Chris

Language differences abound, but this sentiment is clear. When the Irish say 'Fáilte', they mean welcome. Pictured above: the stone near Lisanisk Lake, welcoming visitors to Carrickmacross.

# Taking Tea

The Irish are famous for many drinks- Guinness and whiskey to be sure, but the most ubiquitous drink of all is tea. No visit to Ireland is complete without a 'wee dribble' of tea. It warms you on a raw day and gives an excuse to put your feet up and relax. In fact, after any kind of mishap or accident, what more civilized way to soothe the nerves than a restorative cup of tea ?

Years ago when I went visiting I was always served whiskey first and then tea to follow, but the Irish are much more concerned about drinking and driving than they used to be, and so that custom has changed a bit. Still, being invited to tea rarely means just a quick cuppa. Tea, which may be served anywhere from late afternoon to evening, is most often what I would call a meal. We had tea with grilled rashers (bacon) and tomatoes, tea with ham sandwiches and potato salads (which might be any salad with a mayonnaise type dressing), and tea with beets, salads, and chicken wings. A whole array of breads and scones round out the meal, including my favorite, Irish brown bread. Of course, no tea would be complete without biscuits (cookies) and a cake, a torte or a flan. Some days we had tea with one relative after another, and returned home awash with tea and delighted by the Irish hospitality.

Left: Clockwise from top- Tea at the Ballymascanlon Hotel, a lovely torte, a picnic tea in Carlingford with Lisa and Denise
Top: Terri and Chris at tea with the relatives
Right: Tea at a neighbor's house in Rosslough.

After totally ruining both tires on the passenger side of our rental car, we stopped for a much needed, soothing tea at the the Ballymascanlon House Hotel. The name, meaning 'the town of the son of Scanlon' may seem a mouthful, but the hospitality is worth every syllable. Here the desk clerks helped us call a garage and invited us to relax in the tea room while our tires were replaced.

Located on the Cooley Peninsula, the Ballymascanlon House Hotel sits on the Scanlon estate dating from 833 CE. The chiefton, MacScanlon, repelled a Danish invasion near here in that year. However, the whole area was historically important long before his time. For instance, the Proleek Dolmen was erected during the Bronze Age, some 4000 years ago. More recently, St. Brigid, the second patron saint of Ireland, was born near here in Faughart circa 453 CE. Easy access to Carlingford, Dublin, Belfast, the Irish Sea, and the Mourne Mountains make this area an ideal launching point for travelers.

Left and Facing Page: Views of Ballymascanlon House Hotel

Note the various different building materials used for the different sections dating from various periods. The smooth yellow stone house is Victorian.

Festina Lente, the motto which is enlarged below, means 'Make Haste Slowly.'

FESTINA LENTE

Top: Thatch roofs are no longer common in Ireland. This one is in Ardee, County Louth. In the Middle Ages, Ardee was a walled town, but little evidence of those walls remains today. The four-day, single-combat battle between Cúchulainn and Ferdia took place in Ardee.

Above left: A wall in Stonetown          Above right: A pub/shop at an intersection in Louth Village

# County Louth

**C**ounty Louth, where Dad lived for over twenty years, is the smallest county in the Republic of Ireland, but the second most densely populated. Its capital, Dundalk, is north of Dublin. County Louth draws a number of tourists each year in part because of its rich history. Named for the Irish god, Lugh (Lú), the father of the famous hero, Cúchulainn, the county is the setting for the legendary Táin Bó Cúailnge (see pages 68 ff). The area has seen more than its share of invaders, including Vikings, Scots, English, and Normans. Reminders of these multiple layers of history can be found in the many ruins throughout the county.

Above: Ardee Castle (actually a fortified tower house) was built in the fifteenth century and used as a prison in the seventeenth and eighteenth centuries.
Right: St. Mochta's House. Legends claim this house was built in a single night to house St. Mochta, a sixth century disciple of St. Patrick. However, this structure dates from the twelfth century. St. Mochta's House is located just outside of Louth Village, a rural community near my dad's home in Rosslough.

Left and Above: Two views of the east gable wall of St. Mary's Augustinian Priory. At nearly 151 feet long, St. Mary's is thought to be the longest church in Ireland. The priory is on the site of St. Mochta's sixth century monastery.

Above and facing page: The South wall of St. Mary's Augustinian Priory, Louth Village, County Louth.
St. Mochta's monastery was built on this location in 528 CE. None of the original buildings of that monastery remain following multiple raids by Vikings and various Irish kings. The first ill-fated St. Mary's Priory was built here in the 1130's. However, a storm and no fewer than seven fires completely ruined that original monastery by 1166. The current structure was built in the thirteenth century, long after the last fire. After churches were repressed during the Reformation, the priory became part of the Church of Ireland, but fell into ruins from the seventeenth century battles of the rebellion. The crumbling walls still standing only hint at the beauty that once graced this remarkable priory.

Top: The west gable end of St. Mary's Priory.

Bottom: A stone wall and rusted iron gatework enclosing an area of graves within St. Mary's Priory ruins.

# Mellifont Abbey

Since St. Patrick brought Christianity to Ireland in the fifth century, that religion has been an important part of the fabric of Irish life. Evidence of this early importance can be seen in the high stone crosses, the monastic towers, and the magnificent abbeys throughout the land. Even though many of these have fallen into ruin after King Henry VII dissolved all of the Irish monasteries, their presence remains. One such religious monument is Mellifont Abbey, which is located in County Louth, approximately ten kilometers to the northwest of Drogheda, less than an hour's drive north of Dublin. Mellifont Abbey was built on the banks of the River Mattock in the style of contemporary French abbeys, with romanesque arches and impressive stonework. Though it is mostly in ruins today, in its heyday, it must have been beautiful.

Called An Mhainistir Mhór --the big abbey-- in Irish, Mellifont means 'fount of honey' in Latin. It was founded in 1142 by St. Malachy, the Archbishop of Armagh. St. Malachy thought the monastic orders in Ireland at the time were lax and disorganized, so he established Mellifont Abbey as a Cistercian abbey. Cistercian monks were well known as hard-working and pious. Indeed, the abbey quickly prospered. It became the biggest, most important abbey in Ireland, hosting kings, bishops, and papal legates at the

1152 synod. By 1170, one hundred monks and at least three hundred lay brothers lived there. Eventually, over twenty 'daughter' abbeys were established by monks from Mellifont Abbey throughout Ireland.

Unfortunately, the abbey's wealth led to its downfall. King Henry was suspicious of that wealth and the power attending it. He dissolved the abbeys in Ireland in 1539. Mellifont Abbey became a fortified manor owned by various different families. William of Orange even used it for his battle headquarters during the Battle of the Boyne in 1690.

I visited the ruins of Mellifont Abbey many years ago on a drizzly day-- typical Irish weather. There were few other visitors that day, and we enjoyed strolling along the gravel walkways between the stone foundations which marked the layout of the original buildings. At one end of the complex is the lavabo. The lavabo was a washroom, used by the monks for ritual (and practical) hand-washing before eating. Though it too is in ruins, three of the original eight beautiful Romanesque arches remain. Some of the ornate carvings from the lavabo and other buildings are displayed in the visitor center.

It seems fitting somehow that this spiritual place of cleansing has in some part outlasted the depredations of time, wars, and human greed. Though the place is deserted now, when I closed my eyes and listened, I could imagine the splash of water and the footfalls of the monks as they washed their hands, in a time-honored (and scientifically supported) ritual of purification.

Left: Looking out from the inside of the lavabo.
Above: Remains of some Abbey walls with the lavabo in the background.

# Carrickmacross and County Monaghan

**M**y father lived in nearby Roslough, County Lough, but my relatives all live in and around Carrickmacross in parishes with lovely names that roll trippingly off the tongue, like Lisnagunnion where my great-grandfather was born, and Donaghmoyne, where my parents are now buried.

Although people lived in the area much earlier, Carrickmacross developed as a market town in the seventeenth century, when Queen Elizabeth granted a barony to the Earl of Essex. His castle, burnt down in 1641, was situated where the Convent of St. Louis now stands. For many years, Carrickmacross had the only pig market in the area. (See page 13 for a picture of the market tollhouse.) With a population of just over 5,000 in 2016, the town is a very friendly and welcoming place.

Left: The steeple of St. Joseph's in Carrickmacross, built in 1866
Above Left: Carrickmacross Library Square          Right: Main Street in Carrickmacross

Carrickmacross is well known for the beautiful, handmade lace made and sold here. In 1820 Mrs. Grey Porter, wife of the rector of Donaghmoyne, devised a scheme to help women earn a bit of extra money. This enterprise met only limited success, but during the Great Famine in 1846, the Bath and Shirley Estates established a lace making school to help their starving tenants. From these beginnings, Carrickmacross lace has become well-known worldwide. However, this cottage industry nearly disappeared toward the end of the nineteenth century due in part to deteriorating designs, lack of patronage, and declining demand for handmade lace. The Sisters of St. Louis revived the tradition by establishing the St. Louis Lace School in 1898. They ran the cooperative for nearly one hundred years. In 1987 the sisters turned over the lace making enterprise to the Carrickmacross Lace Co-Op, which still operates to this day.

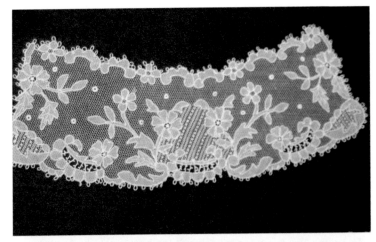

Right page: Lace samples. Carrickmacross handmade lace comes in a variety of styles and shapes, from Christmas ornaments and bookmarks to Communion veils and christening gowns. Designers for Queen Victoria's wardrobe often ordered Carrickmacross lace. Princess Diana's wedding dress also featured Carrickmacross lace.

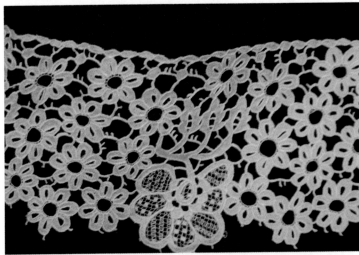

One soft day in 2007, my cousin Maura took me on a driving tour of the Lisnagunnion-Donaghmoyne area, sharing places that were important to her family over the years. These are the places not meant for toursits, but for the ordinary Irish people.

Top: The old Lisdoonan dance hall, now abandoned.

Bottom: Lisdoonan National School (Elementary grades)

Top: A mass rock used as an altar. During Cromwell's rule and the Penal Laws of the seventeenth century, celebrating Catholic mass was illegal. Such rocks are found in rural areas throughout Ireland. Often the rock was taken from a Catholic church that had been ruined. Mass was unscheduled and notice of the service was spread by word of mouth among the congregation. By the eighteenth century, these clandestine masses were more often held in parishioners' homes. This mass rock sits in a field above my relatives' homes in the Lisnagunnion-Donaghmoyne area.

Bottom: St. Mary's Church, Lisdoonan, was built in 1812 without a belfry. This cast iron, freestanding bell was erected in 1920.

51

Shirley Arms Hotel.
The Shirley Family was one of the major landholders in the Carrickmacross area, having inherited the estate from the Earl of Essex when he died without an heir in 1646. The hotel on the grounds of the former estate has been at this location since 1821.

Above: This Carrickmacross cottage sits on the road by St. Joseph's, near the cottages built on St. Joseph's Terrace, which was part of the Bath Estate. The Thynne family, later Marquesses of Bath, were the second largest landowners in the area, having shared in the inheritance of the Earl of Essex, along with the Shirley family. The building on the right is one of the Weymouth Cottages built between 1865 and 1875.

Inniskeen is a village in County Monaghan near the border of County Louth. The Irish name (Iniscaoin) means 'peaceful island', though that designation is not to be taken literally as the village is not an actual island.

Top: This round tower is all that is left of the sixth century monastery established here by Saint Daith. Vikings plundered the monastery in 948 CE.

Below: This silhouette statue of Patrick Kavanagh shows him at ease. He was one of Ireland's greatest poets. He was born in Inniskeen in 1904 and is buried here with his family.

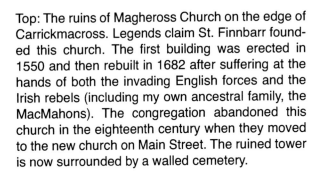

Top: The ruins of Magheross Church on the edge of Carrickmacross. Legends claim St. Finnbarr founded this church. The first building was erected in 1550 and then rebuilt in 1682 after suffering at the hands of both the invading English forces and the Irish rebels (including my own ancestral family, the MacMahons). The congregation abandoned this church in the eighteenth century when they moved to the new church on Main Street. The ruined tower is now surrounded by a walled cemetery.

Bottom: A close-up view of the Magheross Church tower. Note that the Irish for Magheross is *Mhachaire Rois* (wooded plain) and Carrickmacross is *Carraig Mhachaire Rois* (rock of the wooded plain).

Carrickmacross Fever Hospital: In 1842, when the Fever Hospital was built, most doctors and nurses had little training. This hospital treated patients with TB, Typhoid fever, smallpox, and pneumonia, among other ailments. The Fever Hospital once cared for Patrick Kavanagh, a famous poet from nearby Inniskeen, when he had typhoid fever. The Hospital remained open until the 1950's. A few years after that, it became a jam factory for awhile, and was later used for office spaces.

Carrickmacrosss Workhouse: (in Irish: *Teach na mBocht* or Poor House)
This workhouse was built in the same style as many of the over 130 workhouses built in Ireland in the 1840's. The building was capable of housing 500 people. After the contracts were signed in 1840, the actual building began. The first paupers were housed here in 1843. A children's wing providing housing and a school room was added in 1851. The Potato Famine was one reason there were so many starving, destitute people in Ireland at this time. The workhouse closed in 1921 and served as a technical school for awhile. Having undergone some restorations, the workhouse is currently open for tours.

# Carlingford and Environs

In a land full of legends, Carlingford and the Cooley Peninsula offer some of the finest. Carlingford sits on the banks of Carlingford Lough, a fjord serving as the northern border of the Republic of Ireland. This northeast corner of County Louth combines a rich historical heritage with stunning views of the Cooley and Mourne Mountains. Located approximately halfway between Dublin and Belfast, Carlingford has been occupied at least since the Viking invasions of the ninth century. The town of Carlingford itself is Ireland's best preserved medieval village, and the home of the famous Oyster Festival held each August. My sisters and I spent a day there and could easily have spent a week.

Left: The Thosel Gate, one of the few remaining town gates in Ireland. Such gates controlled goods coming into the city to make sure merchants paid all taxes due. The Thosel Gate was used as a jail in the eighteenth century and remodeled in the nineteenth century.
Top: Carlingford Lough
Above Right: Thosel Street in Carlingford, open for pedestrians

My dad tells a story of the farmers in the hills around Carlingford. Several years ago, there was an outbreak of foot-and-mouth disease among the sheep. Even now there is no effective vaccine to control the infection. Many farmers in the region share pasturage and so the only way to contain this highly infectious scourge was to cull all infected or exposed animals, resulting in the loss of the whole herd. One farmer reported a loss of 700 ewes, 500 lambs, and 35 rams. With other farmers losing a similar number of sheep, you can imagine it was a devastating economic setback for the entire area.

In an effort to control the outbreak and encourage compliance, the government paid the farmers a small compensation for shooting their stock. In order to figure out how much each farmer should get paid, the government workers were supposed to count the sheep. Remember, the Cooley Peninsula has rough terrain, with steep, rocky hillsides. The story goes, the government workers were reluctant to climb the hills to count the sheep, so they counted them from the roadside down below the fields. The area farmers, quick to find a silver lining in a bad situation, painted the rocks to look like sheep. Apparently the ruse worked well enough to earn the farmers a bit more compensation and a reputation for cleverness.

Below: One of the many sheep in the hills around Carlingford

Sheep are not the only inhabitants of the Cooley Peninsula. Allegedly, the last of Ireland's Leprechauns live in the hills above the town. In fact, in 2009, the Leprechauns' mountain home was declared a preserve by the European Union Habitats Directive and Leprechauns are listed as a protected species, since their existence, while not proven, has also not been disproved.

The discovery of the local Leprechauns is attributed to P. J. O'Hare, who found a small green suit and hat, a small skeleton, and four gold coins on Slieve Foy (Foy Mountain) in 1989. Some people believed him, but others didn't. One of his friends, McCoilte, wanted to test the issue. He arranged a Leprechaun hunt. Ahead of the hunt, he hid five ceramic statues of Leprechauns, with 1000 Irish pounds under each. He sold Leprechaun hunting licenses and figured the prize money would act as an incentive to hunt the wary creatures. With so many people hunting the ceramic Leprechauns, someone was bound to find any real Leprechauns in the area. Though the hunt continues to be held yearly (with different prizes as time has passed), no one has yet sighted a Leprechaun. But McCoilte, an early skeptic, became a believer when he met a Leprechaun named Carraig. According to McCoilte, Carraig said the demise of the Leprechauns was caused by the lack of belief in them (just as Tinkerbell claims in Peter Pan). In addition to the annual Leprechaun Hunt, Carlingford now has a Leprechaun and Fairy Cavern for visitors to learn more about the wee creatures.

Left: This Leprechaun door, near St. John's castle, is less than a foot high.

A much older legend from pre-Christian days concerns the Irish hero, Finn McCool (Fionn mac Cumhaill in Irish) and the Cloughmore Stone (pronounced clock-more). There are many stories involving Finn, an important mythical Irish warrior and hero. In this story, Finn was out hunting one day. After a long, hard chase, he killed a giant wild boar at the top of Slieve Foy, the highest of the Cooley Mountains. As Finn was roasting the animal over a nearby volcano, a giant nearly as large as himself stood on the opposite side of the Carlingford Lough.

The sun glinted off this giant's shining helmet. He carried a white shield, a club, and broad sword, called a claideamh.

"Who are you?" Finn shouted to the interloper.

"My name is Ruscaire, and I am the giant of snow and ice, the cock of the north, and the enemy of all human-kind." He raised his club. "And this is Thrasher, ready to smite any who challenge me. And who are you, little man?" With this he began crowing like the rooster he claimed to be. He flapped his arms as if they were wings.

Finn was greatly annoyed by this insult. "I am the giant of summer, the protector of mankind. Roosters may crow on top of the dung heap and you are no better than that. Stop that infernal crowing at once, or I shall come over there and put a stop to it myself."

"If it's fighting you want," roared Ruscaire, "then it's fighting you shall have."

The two giants drew their swords. They hacked and slashed at each other from dawn until dusk and into the night, with neither gaining the advantage. The next day they fought with clubs, but neither could prevail against the other. Finally, exhausted, they each took a break on their own side of the Carlingford Lough.

That night as Finn lay sleeping, Ruscaire snuck up on him and stole his mighty sword. Though he could have slain Finn in his sleep, Ruscaire refrained from such a cowardly trick.

When Finn woke the next morning and found his sword gone, he flew into a great rage. He picked up one of the boulders near him and threw it across the lough at Ruscaire. Ruscaire answered in kind and so began the battle of rocks and boulders. The giants heaved the boulders across the lough as if they were pebbles. and the great stones crashed upon the mountains, shaking them like massive earthquakes.

As the boulders rained down around him, Finn grew angrier and angrier. At last he seized the Cloughmore Stone from the side of Slieve Foy. He hoisted this fifty ton rock to his shoulder, and then with great effort hurled it toward Ruscaire. The boulder landed on the winter giant's head, and crushed him into the mountain. Ruscaire's body melted away under it like thawing ice and the giant was seen no more. And so the Cloughmore Stone remains on the north side of the lough to this day.

Meanwhile, Finn was thoroughly exhausted by his long battle with Ruscaire. He lay down to rest on the mountains, using the peak as a pillow for his head and letting his feet slide down into the lough. He slept on and on.

In fact, he was so tired, he has never yet woken. Gradually the trees and grasses have grown over him. Sheep graze in the meadows covering the giant, and red deer, foxes, and pine martens make their home along his broad back. Soothed by the lullabies of the curlews, plovers, and cuckoos, the giant Finn McCool, his body now turned to stone, still sleeps beneath the Cooley mountains.

Above: Looking north, across the Carlingford Lough

In addition to the Thosel town gate mentioned previously, Carlingford boasts three more medieval structures. The largest of these is **Taaffe's Castle** (left), as it is called today, near the center of town. This castle was built in the early sixteenth century as a fortified tower home and safe depository for the Taaffes, a rich merchant family. Though it is now in ruins, in its prime, the castle was four stories tall with a roof walk and a turret. It is likely that the ground floor was used for busines and the upper levels were living spaces. Theobald Taaffe became the first Earl of Carlingford in 1661.

In recent years, the building has been used as a pub. The place even claims its own ghost, a headless figure in white. She's said to be a servant girl who was about to marry Nicholas Taaffe. He went off to fight in the Battle of the Boyne in 1690. He was killed in battle and beheaded. She mysteriously suffered the same fate and now haunts the castle halls. Other versions of the story claim that it is Nicholas himself who roams the castle.

An older structure, **Carlingford Castle** (right), dominates the north edge of town. This castle was built near the end of the twelfth century by Hugh deLacy, a Norman Baron. At first, King John of England favored Hugh. But when Hugh became too powerful, King John seized the castle from him in 1210. It is possible King John visited or stayed in the castle for a short time, which is why it is often called King John's Castle. The castle offers a strong point of defense, but by 1549 it was in bad condition. At some point in its history, cannons had been fired against it. Some of the cannon balls have been found in the ruins. The whole castle was abandoned in the eighteenth century. Recently it has been renovated to make it open to the public.

The third important medieval building in Carlingford is the **Mint**, a three-story fortified tower house (shown above). It was built in the fifteenth or sixteenth century, probably for a rich merchant family, although it is not known for whom. As a fortified tower house, the Mint has battlements, musket loopholes, and even a machicolation above the doorway. However, it does not have a fireplace, which would be expected in a fortified house. Although Carlingford was granted the right to mint coins in 1467, this building was probably never used as a mint. No coins minted in Carlingford have ever been found. In the absence of a stable police force and rule of law, these rich merchants needed a strong hold to protect their wealth just lke the Taaffe family.

The most remarkable features of the Mint are the five ogee windows which face the street.

An ogee window is a window with a mirrored double curve arch. as seen on this page and the facing page. The limestone on these windows is beautifully carved, with fancy hood mouldings and mullions. Shown here are some of the designs, including a horse and Celtic knot interlacing. Besides the carvings shown here, the stonework includes a man's bust, a bird, and a snake. The patterns and motifs represent Celtic Restoration Art of the sixteenth century.

# Táin Bó Cúailnge

The hills around Carlingford are particularly well-known for hiking, or hill-walking as they say in Ireland. One such hike, the Táin Way, follows the path of the great Irish epic, the Táin Bó Cúailnge'. Translated, this means, 'the driving off of the cows of Cooley', but it is more commonly referred to as the Cattle Raid of Cooley. The story is written in a combination of prose and poetry spoken by some of the characters within the story. Sometimes called the Irish National Epic, this tale has had tremendous influence on Irish literature. It tells of the war between the forces of Queen Medb of Connacht and the hero, Cúchulainn of Ulster. Queen Medb had a tremendously fertile bull in her herd. However, the bull did not want to be owned by a woman, and joined Medb's husband's herd. This meant Medb was less wealthy than her husband by one great bull. So she gathered her great army and set out to steal the Brown Bull of Cooley (Donn Cúailnge) from Ulster. Because the men of Ulster had been disabled by a mysterious illness, the god/hero Cúchulainn fought for them. After a great many battles, single combats, tricks, and subterfuges, with help from various gods and supernatural figures on both sides, the bull was badly wounded and wandered around Ireland before finally dying. Much of the action of this national epic takes place in and around the Cooley Peninsula.

Our story of the Táin is more mundane--a story like many of my stories of getting lost and finding the way. My sisters and I spent a few hours hiking a small part of the 25 mile loop of the Táin Way, starting in Carlingford. To begin,

we went up a very steep paved road, which led to a grassy path. This was a lovely track, winding past stone-walled fields with grand views of the harbor and city below. At one point the track runs alongside a conifer forest that looks like a forest where one might find Robin Hood and his band of men. Though armed with a map that I bought for 7.50 Euros, we found it difficult at times to tell the difference between a cow path in a farmer's field and a National Waymarked Trail. Our map had no scale and things marked on the map rarely corresponded to the things we saw. As we went on, the track narrowed. We crossed a creek and a muddy rivulet. We were looking for a place the track should turn downhill, and circle back into the town, but we couldn't find it. We saw a

Views along a section of the Táin Way above Carlingford

latched gate we thought might be right, but couldn't tell if it led into a farmer's field or not. We went on another couple of kilometers with no better luck. Eventually we decided to turn back the way we had come and try the latched gate. This path was quite overgrown in places and looked as if it had rarely been used in the last decade. At times the way was four to five feet wide, but in other places it was barely the width of a single person. Stone or wire fences ran along the sides of it. We trekked along a stone wall that might have been built in the middle ages, through a swampy rill where the trail shrank to less than a foot wide, and eventually found our way back to town near King John's castle.

Above: The Táin Way winds through farmlands, fields, and forests. This picture is part of the trail that is easy to follow.
Left top: In places the path was lined with a stone wall, much like many of the roads criss-crossing Ireland.
Left bottom: My sisters, Denise and Chris, are ready to start down this path back to town. The only question for us was whether or not this really was the path.

# Proleek Dolmen

Though perhaps most famous for the saint that drove away the snakes, Ireland has many more ancient mysteries, including nearly 200 portal tombs, often called dolmens or stone tables. Dolmens usually have three or more standing stones with a (more or less) flat capstone resting on top. Usually two of the standing stones form a portal to the inner chamber. Some evidence suggests that the standing stones and table stone were originally covered with a cairn of smaller rocks, so what we see today is only the skeleton of the neolithic structure.

These neolithic monuments are found throughout Europe, Asia, and Africa. Like the more famous Stonehenge, the massive stone monuments have inspired awe in the millennia since they were built. Questions abound. Why were they built? How were they built? Who built them? For the most part, these questions remain unanswered. No one knows for sure why the dolmens were built. Many archaeologists consider these monuments to be single-chamber, megalithic tombs, but there is insufficient evidence to be sure. A more intriguing, though less scientific, explanation can be found in many legends that have been told explaining the dolmens, including stories of giants buried there, sleeping on top, or using the table stone as a griddle.

One delightful example is the Proleek Dolmen found on the grounds of Ballymascanlon House Hotel in County Louth. Built circa 3000 BCE, its portal stones are about three meters (nearly ten feet) high, and the capstone weighs over 35 tons. The portal faces westward, toward Slieve Gullion, so that at the summer solstice it is facing the sunset behind the mountain.

Why it's called the Proleek Dolmen is another mystery. References to this monument in 1895 call it the Puleek Cromleach or Puleek Dolmen. One nickname is the Giant's Load. According to legend, a Scottish giant called Parrah Boug MacShagean carried the stone here. Parrah challenged the famous Irish hero, Finn McCool. Always more ready to trick his opponents than fight them, Finn poisoned the Flurry River which runs nearby. Parrah drank from it and died, leaving Finn the victor. The legend claims that the Scottish giant was buried in the wedge tomb found about 80 meters from the Dolmen.

Legends aside, wedge tombs were generally built 500 to 1000 years after the portal tombs and are unique to Ireland. The wedge tomb here runs west to east. The tomb is formed by two rows of large stones, decreasing in width and height to form a wedge. A single roof stone remains, capping the east end of the tomb. Though not as impressive as the portal tombs, the wedge tombs are still a marvel of neolithic engineering. They are the last of the great megalithic tombs built in Ireland.

Finding the Proleek Dolmen can be an adventure. With little fanfare and few signs to guide the visitors, this 5000 year old monument to human ingenuity sits in a small clearing on the estate grounds. I've been to see the Proleek Dolmen a couple of times on my visits to Ireland, since it is in the same county where my Dad lived. The most recent was a visit with my three sisters. We arrived on a rainy afternoon after a stressful encounter with Irish roads and ditches. After we indulged in a restorative cup of tea in the hotel dining room, we ambled out through the rose courtyard, through a cattle gate, and alongside the fairway of the hotel golf course, where the intrepid tourist must be aware of stray golf balls. The rain let up by the time we reached the dolmen in a little clearing in the Irish countryside.

Legend says that whoever throws a pebble on top of table stone and gets it to stay there, will either (depending on the version) marry within a year, return to Ireland, or have good luck. Since my sisters and I are already married we hoped for the luck. All of us managed to get the rock to stay on top, though it took me three tries. Perhaps that's enough to guarantee continued good luck. And we all hope to return to Ireland many times.

Above: The wedge tomb on the grounds of Ballymascanlon Holel

Lucky or not, the dolmen is worth the visit. Touching stones lifted into place by nameless hands centuries ago gives a profound sense of awe. Did the builders mourn for their loved ones? Did they believe the dead would live on, perhaps in a better place? There are no answers. Those who were buried beneath the stones, those who built the tomb, those who loved and cared for the dead are all gone now, unknown and perhaps unknowable. Yet the tomb remains, a mystery and an inspiration.

Above: A rose garden on the grounds of Ballymascanlon Hotel

# The Dolmen

## by Valerie Biel

The magic here on misty morns
When the last tendrils of fog are burned away
And the warm sun reveals the ancient portal
Growing out of the turf like a sentinel to the past
A doorway to the world of eternal slumber
Keeping the secrets of the long-ago buried
Noble people who came before us.

# Brú na Bóinne

**I**n 3,200 BCE, before the pyramids were built in Giza or Stonehenge was built in England, a group of farmers in the valley of the River Boyne began a daunting project: building a series of massive, chambered cairns. Using stones from as far away as the mountains of Mourne and Wicklow (over sixty miles north and south), they built Newgrange, Knowth, Dowth, Townley Hall, and at least thirty-five other, smaller cairns in the area, collectively known as Brú na Bóinne. Though the great mound at Knowth is older and larger, Newgrange is more famous and is probably the best-known passage tomb in the world, with over 200,000 visitors a year.

The valley of the River Boyne has been a center of civilization from prehistoric times. Even before the great cairns were built, older structures were present at this bend in the Boyne. It's really no surprise the Neolithic farmers built here. The lands around the River Boyne are fertile, and the water of the river is said to bestow knowledge on any who drink from it. Equally important, the river teams with salmon, the fish revered in Irish myth as the symbol of knowledge.

Left: Views of Newgrange
Above: River Boyne near Newgrange          Above Right: The entrance portal for the winter solstice sun

So the mystery is not why the Neolithic farmers built here, but why they built these cairns at all. We still don't know exactly how they were used. This type of monument is called a passage tomb. Such passage tombs were built by Neolithic peoples across Europe and show a stable, well-organized society with enough wealth to devote decades to building. Newgrange probably took twenty to thirty years to build.

A passage tomb has a long underground passage leading to a central chamber. The cremated remains of the dead were placed in the chamber. It's possible that the ashes were placed in the tomb for a period of time and then removed, say at the solstice, but this is speculation without clear evidence.

However, it is clear that the monument at Newgrange was not just a tomb. Archaeologists have suggested Newgrange was a sacred temple used for religious ritual and ceremony. Certainly, the monument was carefully built by people who understood geometry and astronomy. The passage at Newgrange is aligned so the sun comes in over the lintel for five days around the Winter Solstice (December 19-23) each year. At sunrise, a shaft of light streams through the tunnel to the back of the passage. As the sun rises higher, the light widens, illuminating the chamber for about seventeen minutes.

By 2500 BCE, nearly 1000 years after it was built, Newgrange had fallen into disrepair, though it was still revered as a holy place. Sometime around 2000 BCE, long after the Neolithic farmers were gone, Bronze Age people surrounded Newgrange with about thirty-seven menhirs or huge standing stones for their own equally unknown purposes, possibly religious or commemorative in nature. Only twelve of these stones are still there today. As the centuries

Right: A smaller passage tomb mound at Brú na Bóinne, that has not yet been excavated

followed, the people who built the mounds were forgotten and the original purpose was lost, but the place remained sacred, a holy place of mystery.

Later, when the first waves of Celts arrived in Ireland about 500 BCE, the mounds were seen as the homes of their gods, the Tuatha de Danann. The name Brú na Bóinne means 'mansion' or 'palace of the Boann.' Boann, whose name may be translated as milk cow, is the queen goddess of the River Boyne. She is said to have created the river by walking widdershins, or counter-clockwise, around the magical Well of Wisdom. One of the many legends surrounding the monument says Boann lived at Brú na Bóinne with her husband, Elcmar, horse lord of the ancient Tuatha de Danann. Boann fell in love with Dagda (the good god). Dagda tricked Elcmar, sending him on an errand to the king. Elcmar believed he was only gone for a day and night, but in reality, he was gone for nine months, long enough for Boann to become pregnant and deliver Dagda's child. The boy, Aengus Og, represented youth and love. When he grew up, he tricked his father into ceding Brú na Bóinne to him. Soon after that, Aengus fell ill. It turned out he had fallen in love with a girl he saw in his dreams. The girl, Caér, lived in the neighbouring kingdom of Connacht, and her father refused to let her marry Aengus. But the girl was of the race of the gods too and spent alternating years as a bird. Aengus went to her when she was in bird form and called her to him. She agreed to come with him if he promised to allow her to return to the water. He did, and so they both took the form of swans and flew back to Brú na Bóinne, where they lived happily ever after.

Left: These stone menhirs were erected by Bronze Age people nearly 1000 years after the passage tombs were built.

As Ireland became Christianized, the old gods were relegated to stories where they became the fairies or little people of legend, living underground and interacting with the world above. The religious connection died away, but the stories did not. As recently as 40 years ago, I heard a mother warning her seven-year-old daughter not to walk on a fairy mound lest she be taken by the little people. For centuries the mounds were left undisturbed, a place of magic and mystery.

By the twelfth century, Newgrange's entrance had caved in, and the passage and chambers underground were forgotten except in stories. In 1142, Mellifont Abbey was built (see pages 43 ff). The abbey acquired a great deal of land, including the fertile Boyne Valley, with its fields of grass and tree-covered mounds. The place was called 'the new grange'—grange meaning an outlying farm connected to the abbey. When Henry VIII suppressed the monasteries in 1539, the land Mellifont Abbey had owned became available for settlement by English landlords. Over a century later in 1699, one such landlord rediscovered the opening of Newgrange while quarrying. For the next few centuries the place was looted and neglected. Graffiti inside the passage even shows the presence of Victorian tourists.

In 1882 the site became protected, but excavation did not begin until 1962. At that time the cremated remains of five bodies were found in the tomb, but since the tomb had been plundered the actual number of people buried there remains unknown. Brú na Bóinne became a World Heritage site in 1997.

Like those early Victorian tourists, I was drawn to Newgrange by the legends of the little people and the otherworldly aura. Today, getting there is relatively easy, as long as you do not follow the signs in Slane pointing to Newgrange. These signs point the way to the old entrance, which is no longer accessible. Newgrange itself is on the north side of the river, while the visitor center through which one gets access is on the south side. The closest bridge across the river is in Slane. Irish GPS (or Sat Nav) still

directs travellers to the monument itself, not the visitor center. On our last visit, my sisters and I did not know this. After wandering the back roads surrounding Slane for hours, we stopped and asked a kind, old gentleman for directions. The old man, who might have been one of the little people for all we knew, began his directions with "You can't get there from here," and ended with "You can't miss it," a sure sign for alarm in any set of directions. He talked earnestly at us for a good ten minutes, giving all sorts of helpful advice, including instructions to cross an iron bridge and digressions about the River Boyne. He explained at length where to find Newgrange, which was really just over the hill. He told us to go down to the bottom of the road and turn right. We thanked him and carried on in somewhat of a daze. Eventually we arrived at what must surely have been the bottom of the road, since it ended. There was a sign directing us to the left for Newgrange Monument. We remembered that the old man had clearly told us to turn right. Since we couldn't remember much of anything else he said, we believed the sign and went left. We drove on and on and on, and eventually arrived back in Slane, where we had started. We found a bridge to cross, though it was not iron but beautiful arched stone, built in the eighteenth century. Once on the correct side of the river, it was fairly easy to follow the river to the Brú na Bóinne Visitor Centre.

Today, Newgrange resembles a huge, circular earth house or perhaps a giant Hobbit hole. It's ninety-three yards in diameter and covers nearly an acre. The walls, about thirty-nine feet high, are made from a milky-white quartz interspersed with grey, river-tumbled cobbles. The mound is capped with a thick mat of green grass. Ninety-seven kerb stones, from about five to fifteen feet in length, surround the base. These big stones are decorated with fascinating megalithic art as enigmatic as the rest of the building. According to our guide 'megalithic art' means 'art on a big rock.'

The best example of megalithic art here is the entrance stone (facing page) with five beautiful, wavelike spirals covering the face of the five-tonne stone. These spirals (below) are often associated with Celtic design but predate the Celts by many centuries. While spirals are a universal, ancient symbol, these three-legged spirals called triskele are unique to the passage tomb builders. Some have said the spirals represent maps or music. Others claim they are symbols of the changing seasons. Still others claim the spirals were used to focus meditation. Most often, triskele are thought to represent life, death, and rebirth, or earth, the spirit world, and beyond. However, they might be purely decorative. With no historical record of the people's thoughts and dreams, it is impossible to know what they meant.

Inside the cairn a low, narrow passageway, sixty-three feet long, slopes upward. Because the passage has a low ceiling forcing visitors to walk slightly stooped, the slope of the passage is not obvious. The passage leads to an inner chamber with three alcoves in the shape of a cross, another ancient symbol. At the center of the cross, the ground is level with the roof box at the entrance. The left leg of the cross has a flat stone basin about three feet across with the most decorations, including a fern. The fern possibly represents the earth. The top leg of the cross has another basin, now broken. More spirals decorate the ceiling. They may represent sky. The ceiling of the vault is a corbelled roof of overlapping stones, each

83

one angled or tilted just slightly by filler rocks so rain seeping through the mound runs out and not into the chamber. The right alcove has two stone basins, one more circular set inside the larger, bottom rectangular basin. Like so many other unanswered questions, the purpose of these basins remains unknown, though they may have been used to hold the cremated remains of important people.

The earth's axis has tilted in the last 5000 years, so the spear of light is no longer exactly centered in the top leg of the cross. It is expected that the light will be re-aligned in about 2000 years. Our guide told us that many of the people at Newgrange were looking forward to that day.

Entrance to Newgrange at the Winter Solstice is quite limited and determined by lottery. For the average visitor entering the tomb at other times of the year, the experience of the solstice is recreated artificially. First all the lights are shut off. Standing in utter darkness, I felt disconnected, separated by more than tons of rock and stone from the real world above me. I could imagine a mystical 'other' world, far older than the one I know. Gradually a thin beam of electric light moved down the passage, growing stronger until it reached nearly to the end of the furthest alcove. For a moment no one breathed, caught in the magic of clear light. Then the guide flipped the switch to turn the electricity back on and we returned to the modern world, emerging with a greater understanding of the skill of these ancient people.

But we are no closer to understanding why the Neolithic passage tomb builders built such monuments. Various people have put forward many theories. There is some evidence the cave was associated with a womb, thus leading credence to the idea the monument represented the concept of life after death. Or perhaps the monument was a way to 'capture' the sun's light on the shortest day of the year, and thus initiate the season where the days begin to lengthen again. There is no way of knowing exactly what the builders were thinking. We have only legends to hint at possibilities.

As my sisters and I left Brú na Bóinne, we paused for a moment on the footbridge crossing the River Boyne. Below us, a cow sipped at the water's edge, and a pair of swans floated side by side. Boann, the milky cow of the Boyne? The lovers, Aengus and Caér?

Perhaps. Likely we will never solve the mystery of these great chambered cairns. But we have the stories.

# The Darkest of Places
## by Barbara Olic-Hamilton

Built of quartz and granite,
buried under dirt,
Newgrange flaunts
a necklace of ninety-seven kerbstones
covered with chiseled tri-spirals.

Wrapped in a darkness
more ancient than the pyramids
and thicker than time,
is a world beyond sunlight's reach.
Weak spring light only
melts the snow on the Entrance Stone.
Long summer days only
glisten on the white quartz
around the entrance opening.
Fall sunsets only
lick the edges
of the roof-box opening.

Inside, a narrow passage burrows
between five thousand year old stones
into a cross-shaped chamber
sitting like a peach stone
surrounded by tattooed rock.

The chamber's darkness is deeper than death,
untouched by sunlight until
the rising sun of Winter Solstice
pushes a needle of sunlight
through the roof-box opening,
threads its thin light along the passageway
between guardian stones,
crosses the chamber floor,
and pools on the basin stone.
Fifteen minutes of sunlight
warms stones cold with the year's darkness,
old with the year's blindness.

Standing in its dark center in February
I can only imagine
that sharp knife of solstice light
cutting into this darkest of places,
promising more light
in this darkest of times.

Cnoc na Teamhrach
by Terri Karsten

A moaning wind
Echoes the haunting bagpipes of old
Evoking a procession of long-dead kings
Swirling skirted warriors
Raise shining spears,
Piercing a cloud-studded sky before
Fading soundlessly beneath the waving grasses.

Above: The Mound of the Hostages, so named from the practice of Irish kings taking hostages to stabilize their rule and solidify their power. However, this mound is really a passage tomb, predating Irish kings by hundreds of years. It is one of only two excavated areas in the hill of Tara complex.

# The Hill of Tara

**O**n a clear, summer day, climb to the top of the Hill of Tara. It is said that one quarter of all Ireland can be seen from this vantage point. A meandering line of silver marks the River Boyne in the valley below. To the east the Irish Sea catches the light. With the great sky opening overhead, and the rolling hills tumbling down from the top, the Hill of Tara seems an empty place. On the day I visited, few tourists wandered the hundred-acre site. Most of the ancient buildings are long gone, their timbers rotted and turned to dust over the millennia, their stone walls buried and forgotten for centuries.

And yet, there is a sense of awe about this place. Close your eyes a moment and feel the brisk wind whipping through the grasses, whispering of ancient power and wisdom and magic. It is this whisper-

Above: This cross commemorates the 1798 Battle of Tara Hill between British forces and Irish rebels. When the rebels lost, it meant the end of the rebellion in County Meath.

Above Right: The actual meaning of this pillar is unknown. Some believe it is the Stone of Destiny, Lia Fáil, used to crown the kings of Ireland. It is said to have been brought here as one of the four treasures of the Tuatha de Danaan, the old gods. It is also said that if the true king stands upon it, the stone will roar. The current placement on the Hill of Tara is not its original position there. The stone was moved in the nineteenth century.

ing that marks the Hill of Tara as sacred. Centuries of human monuments to this mystical feeling lie ruined or buried beneath the sod. From the huge standing stones to the Roman coins found there, the Hill of Tara is one of those places on earth where the aura of the past remains as a powerful force today.

The Hill of Tara, where archaeology and mythology are inextricably entwined, has long been famous as an important historic and prehistoric site in Ireland. Even though most buildings remain unexcavated, archaeologists have found evidence of perhaps a hundred monuments in the Hill of Tara complex. The oldest monument known so far is the neolithic Hill of Hostages, a passage tomb dating to about 3000 BCE. A bonfire lit on this hill on the holy days (such as the solstices, equinoxes and quarter days) could be seen for miles in any direction. (Indeed, the name of Tara comes from the Gaelic Cnoc na Teamhrach (or Temair), usually translated as the 'hill of great prospect'.)

Tara is considered the seat of the high king of Ireland. One famous upright stone at Tara is the Lia Fail, known as the Stone of Destiny. The stone is said to cry out when touched by the rightful high king of Ireland. In fact, the Hill of Tara has seen at least 142 kings crowned.

One such king was Cormac mac Airt, who supposedly built a great hall and a palace on the Hill of Tara. Though there are many legends surrounding him and blurring the truth, Cormac is generally considered to have been a real person, living around the third century CE. It is said that his reign was a time of great peace, when even minor crimes were rare. Some legends claim Cormac is the author of the famous Brehon Laws, which comprise some of the fairest law codes of that or any era. These laws, though maintaining a patriarchal society, afforded some protection of women's rights. Women were free to pursue any profession and could divorce their husbands. Women also were considered partners, not property, in a marriage and maintained the rights to their own property. (Though Cormac gets credit for these laws, the earliest written forms date from the eighth century, several hundred years after Cormac's reign.)

There are many legends regarding the settlement of Ireland. In one, the Tuatha de Danaan, a pre-Celtic people (Children of the Goddess, Dana) defeated the earlier settlers, and made Tara a sacred place to their own gods and goddesses. The Tuatha were in turn defeated by Celtic tribes (e.g., The Milesians) who took over the sacred places, and some of the old rites of the earlier people. The Tuatha were driven underground, becoming the 'little people' of Irish legends. The Hill of Tara remained sacred even into the advent of Christian times. St. Patrick is said to have come to the Hill of Tara in the fifth century CE to preach to King Laoghaire, and convert him and the island to Christianity.

Most of the facts concerning the Hill of Tara are so tangled with legend, we may never know the truth. But this sacred hill where stories live is well worth the visit. All you have to do is listen to the wind and let your imagination soar.

Above: A view of the Boyne Valley from the Hill of Tara.

Above: A view of the Blarney Stone from below. The stone is on the inside of the outer rock framework. The bars were placed later to prevent tourists from falling through the opening as they lay down, leaned backwards over the hole, and kissed the stone.

Facing page, top and bottom: Views of some of the ruins of Blarney Castle.

# Blarney Castle and Grounds

As legends go, it's a pretty weird one. The famous Blarney stone is a large block of limestone set into the far wall of a machicolation high up in Blarney Castle. (A machicolation is a box-like, floorless opening in the battlements, used to pour hot oil or other nasty stuff on intruders.) They say that if you climb to the top of the ruined keep of Blarney Castle, lay down and hang over the edge backwards far enough to kiss that block of limestone set into the battlements, you'll be blessed with the gift of gab. You'll be able to regale audiences with your silvered tongue and eloquence, with the fluency and perhaps even the loquacity to rival the best orators. Having kissed the stone twice myself, I can tell you first hand that the legend is overstated. I'm no orator, and while I can tell a good story, I do better in print than in person.

But if it's all just blarney, why do visitors flock to Blarney Castle every year? The history behind the blarney stone is as nebulous as its purported virtues. One story claims Cliodhna /kleen-a/, a major goddess in the Irish pantheon of the Tuatha de Danann, sometimes known as the Queen of the Banshees or the queen of the Sidheog (fairy women), was involved. Lord MacCarthy, the builder of Blarney castle in 1446 asked for Cliodhna's help to win a lawsuit. She advised him to kiss a stone on his way to court. He did, and then won his case through his eloquent tongue. He then used the special stone in the building of his castle.

A hundred years later, Queen Elizabeth complained of the "blarney" when she could not complete any negotiation with a later McCarthy, the lord of Blarney Castle, because of his noncommittal diplomacy, or the ability to promise little or nothing with a lot of eloquence. While it's true that Cormac McCarthy managed to sweet-talk Queen Elizabeth without signing over his lands, whether his eloquence and wit came from the stone is questionable.

Another early legend says the stone was actually Jacob's pillow and was brought to Ireland by the Prophet Jeremiah. Others say it was part of the 'speaking stone', the throne where Irish kings were crowned at the hill of Tara. Still others claim it was the stone Moses struck in the desert on God's command to bring water to his people. It's even said the stone was the pillow on which St. Columba died.

Only slightly more plausible is the legend of the stone's origin in Scotland. In 1314, before the current Blarney Castle was built, Cormac McCarthy supposedly sent several thousand men to aid Robert the Bruce, and in return Robert gave McCarthy half of the Stone of Scone (or Stone of Destiny), where Scottish kings were crowned.

For the record, all of the legends claiming the stone came from somewhere else have been proved pure blarney by scientific evidence showing the stone to have originated in Ireland. In fact, the Oxford English Dictionary's first recorded use of the term 'blarney' is from 1803, well after Cliodhna and all the early McCarthys slid into oblivion. Perhaps the idea of blarney as lies, half-truths and fabrications all wrapped up in charm came from Lady Blarney, a smooth-talking flatterer in Oliver Goldsmith's *The Vicar of Wakefield,* published in 1766.

Whatever the origins of the stone and the legends surrounding it, the history of Blarney Castle is well-known. The original Blarney castle was built about 1200 AD outside the village of Blarney. Of this first timber structure nothing remains. In 1210, a stone structure was built on the site. This lasted until 1446, when it was destroyed, and the current building was constructed by Cormac Laidir McCarthy. The castle changed hands a number of times in the next several centuries, and eventually fell into disrepair, especially after Blarney House was built in 1874 as a more modern and convenient lodging for the family.

Though it is now mostly in ruins, Blarney Castle and the surrounding gardens are fascinating. It's best to visit early, before the crowds come in. Narrow stone steps, worn smooth with age and use, spiral upward in the dark tower and emerge at the top of the keep. The view over the battlements in the early morning as the mists are rising is as magical as any stone visitors come to kiss. Some of the rooms are still open. Passing through bare stone hallways and into empty rooms, it's easy to imagine the footsteps of the people who lived here hundreds of years ago. In my mind's eye, I could almost see the tapestries warming the walls, the tables laden with roasted game and rich pies, the servants hurrying to fill another goblet. It's as if the stones are whispering their stories, if only we take the time to listen.

Equally enchanting and steeped in legends are the sixty acres of gardens and parklands surrounding the castle. In the Rock Close for instance, moss-shrouded rocks and twisted trees line the meandering paths. In the hush, we could hear the trickle of a waterfall, and when I closed my eyes, I imagined the brush of fairy wings on my cheek. The very air seems steeped with magic. Huge boulders loom over paths winding around an ancient dolmen, a druid's cave, a sacrificial altar, a witch's kitchen, and a stone circle. (These druidic connections were ascribed by the romantic Victorians, without any historical evidence.)

The stone circle called 'The Seven Sisters' has nine huge stones: seven standing and two toppled. In one legend the King of Munster had seven daughters and two sons. When both sons were killed in a battle, the mournful king ordered his men to knock down two of the stones to commemorate his boys.

Another winding path leads to a set of rough stone steps called the wishing steps. According to the legend, anyone who climbs the steps to the stone archway, backwards and with eyes closed, thinking only of their wish, will be granted that wish within a year and a day by the Blarney witch.

From ancient druids to magic stones, from wishing steps and witches to kings of old, Blarney is a place full of stories that stir the imagination. It's a place to make us believe, if only for a moment, that all the legends are true.

Facing page and above: Views of some of the ruins of Blarney Castle.

# Bastions of Safety: A Pair of Irish Castles North and South

**S**ince the dawn of humanity, people have been hard at work trying to keep their homes safe from interlopers. Today, we build fences, lock doors, and install security systems. For the most part, these measures work to keep out the majority of thieves, burglars, and home invaders. But in twelfth century Ireland, with warring chiefs and marauding armies roaming freely, more drastic measures were needed. Their solution? Build a castle. Safety was, after all, the main purpose of a castle.

## Doe Castle

Doe Castle is in Donegal. Like Blarney and many other castles in Ireland, much of Doe Castle is in ruins now, having outlived its usefulness both in battle and as a comfortable home. The moss- and lichen-covered stones of today give little hint of the vibrant life and importance of this castle in the sixteenth century.

Facing page and right: Views of Doe Castle. Round tower walls are stronger than square.
Above: The sea by Doe castle.

It is uncertain exactly when this castle was first built or by whom. Some evidence suggests the castle was there by1425. However, the first actual historical record is from 1549. The area around Doe, with or without the castle, was one of three regions given to the McSweeny clans in 1440, when the Prince of Tyrone and the Prince of Donegal made peace with each other. The name, 'Doe', stems from the Gaelic 'tuath', which means territory or region.

Today, Doe Castle molders in a nearly forgotten corner of Ireland. But before the new road was built in 1849, bypassing the castle access, Doe was in an important strategic position, commanding the surrounding land and sea. For a time the castle was notorious as the venue from which Red Hugh O'Donnell was kidnapped while fostering there. After five years imprisonment in Dublin, Red Hugh escaped and led the O'Donnell clan in their rebellion against the English in the Nine Years War.

As the fighting among the clans and against the English continued during the seventeenth century, the castle passed through many hands, both Irish and English, as alliances changed and battles were won and lost.

By 1700, Doe had faded in importance. Though built to repel invaders, massive stone walls were less effective against the newer technologies of gunpowder and cannon. In addition, with English victories, the fighting died down, leading to greater peace. But squabbles over Doe Castle continued. Several different families and family members claimed ownership over the next century. No one actually lived in the castle after 1843, at least partly because of the cost of repairs and discomfort of the cold and drafty stone walls. By 1932, the Irish Land Comission took over the ownership, and the Castle was listed as a National Monument.

Like many good castles, Doe Castle claims its share of ghosts and their stories. One such example is sung in the ballad, *The Castle of Doe,* written by Niall MacGiolla Bhride (Neil McBride) and published in 1905 in his book of poems called *Heather Blossoms.* The ballad is a tragic love story between Turlough Og O'Boyle and Aileen McSweeney. The two young people met and fell in love in the wild and beautiful hills of Donegal, but Aileen's father, the master of Doe Castle, would not allow their marriage. By means of a small fishing boat, O'Boyle tried to rescue Aileen from her imprisonment in her father's tower. Alas for the lovers, Aileen's father ambushed O'Boyle, captured him, and locked him up in the dungeon. A few days later, he died there in the dark. Poor Aileen saw his corpse carried out of the dungeon on a bier. Heartbroken, she leapt from the tower into the churning sea and drowned. Some claim to see O'Boyle's phantom ship floating over the waves, and in it, the ghosts of Aileen and her lover are united at last.

Left: The battlements of Doe Castle featuring crenellations and machicolations. This is the tower from which Aileen McSweeney was said to have leapt to her death.

# Cahir Castle

Cahir Castle, in County Tipperary, is a prime example of a large, defensive castle. From the earliest times, roving bands of warriors knew that the high ground, with a commanding view of the region, offered the greatest safety because of its defensibility. The site of Cahir Castle on an elevated island in the River Suir offered such a location. The rocky formation also prevented undermining, or tunneling under the castle walls.

In fact, the Irish word 'Cahir' comes from the older word, 'cathair' which means 'fortress.' Even before a castle was built on the huge rock, there was a circular stone fort there. In 1142, Conor O'Brien, Prince of Thomond, built the first actual castle atop the earlier fortifications. A medieval town grew up around the castle.

Over the next 200 years, the Norman Invasion changed the political landscape of Ireland. Finally, in 1375 James Butler was awarded the new title of Baron of Cahir and given the castle as a reward for his loyalty to Edward III. Except for a few brief periods, the castle remained in the Butler family until 1961, when the last heir died and the castle became the property of the state.

James Butler and his descendants enlarged and updated the castle defenses for centuries. During all that time, the castle was lost to the Butler family on three separate occasions, only once by force. The first was in 1599 when most of the Butler family threw in their lot with the Irish against the Earl of Essex' army, sent by Queen Elizabeth. Essex took the castle after a three-day siege, The castle garrison tried to escape. Some did, but many more were slain. The English army took over the castle without further resistance. A year later, 60 Irish rebels took the castle back without gunfire, but they had to surrender shortly thereafter. Thomas Butler was charged with treason, but later he was acquitted and regained his family castle. The castle fell a second time in the Irish Confederate Wars to Oliver Cromwell. In this case, the family managed to regain favor with the crown and took charge of their castle once again. The third time the family lost the castle was due to bankruptcy in the early 1800's. The family was able to buy it back in the 1870's.

Cahir Castle is a model of medieval strongholds. It is considered one of the largest, best preserved, and most impregnable castles in Ireland. It boasts all of the best medieval protective devices including:

- **Batter walls:** stout outer walls that are thicker at the bottom than the top. These walls deflect rocks thrown from the battlements and help prevent tunnelling under the castle to gain entrance.
- **2nd layer of defense**: an inner courtyard, also protected by strong, stone walls. This inner courtyard is only accessible by traversing a long, narrow passageway with a portcullis, making it possible to trap and shoot invaders.
- **Crenellations:** regular rectangular spaces in the stonework along the top of the outer walls, allowing archers to have some protection while shooting. A license from the king was required in order to build crenellations.
- **Loop windows:** long, narrow slits in the castle walls with splayed inner sides allow two defensive archers to shoot at different angles, thus protecting more of the castle wall.
- **Low doors, narrow passages, and stumble steps**: all make it more difficult for strangers to navigate the castle.

Above: The iron portcullis at Cahir Castle.

- **Machicolations**: These openings in the floors above gates and doorways allow the castle defenders to throw down rocks or hot liquids on potential intruders.
- **Portcullis:** a heavy iron grate, often with spiked posts, that can be lowered in a stone gateway to prevent access. The portcullis at Cahir Castle is one of only three working portcullises in Ireland.
- **Spiral Stairs**: These narrow stone stairways are built for a right handed-swordsman to defend against any attackers mounting the stairs.

As in the case of the much smaller Doe Castle, the development of cannons, gunpowder, and other offensive technology, along with a decrease in general warfare, eventually made the elaborate defensive technology of Cahir castle obsolete. Rich families moved into more comfortable dwellings that were built more for beauty than for strength. Cahir Castle, built over 800 years ago to protect the O'Brien and Butler families, is an impressive and stark reminder of the past, when danger threatened just outside a family's gates, and the only protection came from their own strong walls.

# Northern Ireland: The Giant's Causeway

The section of shoreline along the northern coast of Northern Ireland is paved in (mostly) hexagonal stones, laid out like a dance floor for fairies, complete with stepping stones leading from the cliffs and disappearing down into the sea. This natural wonder is known as the Giant's Causeway, a UNESCO world heritage site and a National Nature Reserve in Northern Ireland.

The area looks like it was designed by magical creatures, but science explains that the interlocking basalt columns were formed some 50 to 60 million years ago by volcanic action. The lava from the active volcanoes flowed over the chalk beds. As the lava cooled, it cracked, like drying mud cracks. The cracks extended both horizontally and vertically, forming over 40,000 jointed columns visible today. The columns range from a few feet to over 80 feet high, depending on how fast the lava cooled.

Left: Basalt columns at Giant's Causeway.
Above: Some stepping stones of the giant's bridge.
Right: The giant's eye

101

Though the scientific explanation shows the brilliant complexity of the natural world, it doesn't capture the magic. For that, we need legends. According to the stories I know, the hero, Fionn Mac Cumhaill (or Finn McCool) built a causeway from Ireland to Scotland in order to answer the challenge from the Scottish giant, Benandonner. The task took a week and a day, and when it was finished, Finn was tired and lay down to rest. Finn's wife, Oonagh, saw that fighting was not the best answer. She covered her sleeping husband with a blanket and tied a baby bonnet on his head. When Benandonner came roaring across the causeway looking for Finn, she invited him to sit for tea and wait for Finn to come back from hunting. Benandonner was not happy, but he sat and accepted the tea and cakes. Oonagh told him she had just baked the cakes for the sleeping baby. She didn't tell him she had baked stones in the cakes. When Benandonner bit into one, he broke a tooth.

"Ow," he yelled. "What kind of baby can eat cakes this hard?"

"Hush! You'll wake the baby," Oonagh scolded. She pointed to the cot where Finn was sleeping.

Benandonner was surprised at the size of the baby as he bent over to pat him.

Finn woke up when he felt something tickle his cheek. Thinking it was his wife with a cake, he bit off the end of Benandonner's finger.

Benandonner leapt up. "If this is the baby, I don't want to meet the father!" He ran home, tearing up the causeway as he went so Finn couldn't follow him.

Finn jumped up. He threw great chunks of rock after the fleeing giant. One clump landed in the middle of the channel and became the Isle of Mann. Now, except for that island, only the two ends of the causeway remain, one end in Ireland and the other in Scotland.

I find this story of the Causeway more satisfying than the scientific explanation, in part because it is the clever woman who tricks the giant, and in part because the image of two grown men throwing rocks across the channel reminds me of my toddler grandsons throwing rocks in the pond.

Several unique rock features formed by cooling lava can be found along the shore. They are named to commemorate Finn MacCool's role in the causeway. Look for Finn's Eye, the Giant's Organ, and Finn's Boot, the size of which indicated Finn would have been over 52 feet tall. In the end, whether you clamber over the rocks thinking of the great forces of earth spewing lava that cools and splinters, or you imagine stone-throwing giants or fairies coming to dance, the Giant's Causeway is truly a natural wonder, well worth visiting again and again.

Left and right: views of the Giant's Causeway, including the chimney stacks.

# Giant's Causeway

## by Valerie Biel

Sea-kissed steps to another world
Tempted by the foam that swirled
A giant lured into the fray
Across the waves where selkies play
Bewildered by the giant's size
Finn McCool could only hide
A fight would surely end his life
If not for the ruse of his clever wife
A trick, a bluff, some sleight of hand
Sent the rival back to his land
The bridge destroyed by his hasty flight
Tourists now inspect the site
Wondering if the myth is true
Do giants roam just out of view?

# Northern Ireland: Carrick-á-Rede

Not too far from Giant's Causeway, a wee bit off the north coast of Ireland, is a tiny island, washed by a salty wind, damp and chill from the surrounding sea. Actually, it's more like a big, big rock than a real island. It's called Carrick à Rede, which means either rock in the road, rock of the net, or rock of the bridge, depending on which linguistic evidence is accepted. The island, with its sheer cliffs, black rocks, and barren scrub grass, sits sixty-six feet from the mainland. A rope footbridge, swinging over a hundred foot deep chasm with angry waves swirling over the jagged rocks at the bottom, offers the only way to reach the island.

No one lives on this volcanic plug at this time. It's not big enough, or fertile enough, to support any kind of farm, though there's been a fishery here for four hundred years. A reconstructed stone fisherman's cottage reminds visitors of the island's past. Early fishermen built a bridge from the mainland to the island in the mid-eighteenth century for better access to the great salmon runs in the North Atlantic Ocean by Ballintoy. For most of the 350 years since it

Left: The rope bridge to the island.     Top: Close-up of the rope and thistles
Right: My sister, Lisa, crossing from the mainland.

was built, the bridge was a precarious walk of random planks with only a single rope for a handhold. When I first crossed the bridge back in 1997, there were rope handholds on both sides of the plank walkway, and a rope net for added safety. Since then, the bridge was rebuilt in 2008 with wire rope and steel reinforcements. So there is no danger in crossing now.

But it's still daunting. Sometimes a brave walker makes it to the island, but is too afraid to cross back to the mainland. They must be rescued by helicopter or boat. I don't blame them. I'm not afraid of heights and am rather fond of swinging bridges, even when they bounce a bit from other walkers. Still, I admit to gripping both sides of the rope rail when an unexpected gust of ocean-drenched wind raced through the chasm, and the bridge swayed alarmingly.

Thousands of tourists visit the bridge each year, so many that nowadays you must purchase a timed ticket to cross and the National Trust limits the number of visitors. You might wonder why anyone would want to stand in a long line and pay a fee just to cross a shaky bridge to a barren island so close to the mainland. Part of it is the challenge, of course. Crossing the bridge is a test of courage, a thrill that feels more dangerous than it is. The island itself is beautiful, wind-scoured, and romantic. Tiny wildflowers eek out a hardscrabble existence clinging to the cliff's edge. Seabirds such as razorbills, kittywakes, guillemots, and fulmars screech and circle overhead, their cries nearly drowned by the waves crashing against the volcanic rock. The views northward, across the ocean toward Rathlin Island and Scotland are stunning. Those who wait and watch carefully may even be rewarded with an occasional glimpse of a shark or a dolphin.

Overfishing and changes in migration patterns have made the salmon from this area disappear. The last fisherman left the island in 2002. But the island, carved from the coast by wind and waves thousands of years ago, remains, waiting for those who dare to cross the bridge.

Left: Four sisters on the edge of the island.
Top: Looking down from the top at the historic fisherman's cottage.
Bottom: My sister, Chris, crossing toward the island.

# Wild Ireland: Off the beaten path

Beyond the cities, towns, historic monuments, and castles of Ireland, there are many beautiful places. These are the forests and mountains; the seashores, rivers and lakes; the rolling farmland; and the rugged back roads. In fact, it seems to me just about anywhere I went in Ireland was worthy of a picture. This last chapter captures some of the varied scenery that graces Ireland's countryside, from the majestic to the agrarian, from the well-known to the hidden treasures.

## Conor Pass: Dingle Peninsula

With an elevation of 1,496 feet, Conor Pass features one of the highest paved roads in Ireland. The scenic, one-lane road winds past splashing waterfalls, rocky valleys, and lush green peaks. Driving through this breathtaking scenery is not for the faint-hearted. In addition to the majestic roads, the driver may need to watch for herds of cattle driven along the narrow road, and tour buses, which are not recommended, but still venture the drive. This page and the facing page are all views of Conor Pass

# Slea Head: Dingle Peninsula

Another part of the magnificent Dingle Peninsula is Slea Head (Slí Cheann Sléibhe in Irish), on the southwestern point of the peninsula. Slea Head drive, starting and ending in Dingle, is about 30 miles long. In addition to the beautiful scenery, there are many historic sites along the way, including many stone 'beehive' huts, dating to perhaps the twelfth century. The views on this page and the facing page are from near Slea Head Beach.

# The Burren

The aptly named Burren (Irish *Boirrean*- a rocky place) is a dry, treeless plain in Northwestern County Clare, on the west coast of Ireland. The word 'plain' might be somewhat deceiving, since most of the area has very little topsoil. The landscape, fragmented by cracks and crevices in the karst, looks otherworldy, like something you might find on the moon. Throughout this seemingly empty vista, patches of fertile ground provide habitat for a great variety of plants and animals, some of which are found nowhere else. Fossils, caves, rock formations, ancient stone forts, barrows, and wedge tombs can also be found in the Burren.

# THE CLIFFS OF MOHER

Near the Burren, and part of the Burren-Cliffs of Moher UNESCO Global Geopark are the majestic Cliffs of Moher. With an abrupt cliff edge, these verticle walls soar up to 390 feet above the Atlantic Ocean. Stretching along the coast for over nine miles, the Cliffs of Moher have been one of Ireland's top destinations for tourists since the nineteenth century.

# Dún a Rí

The valley, through which the Cabra River runs, became a park in 1970. The lush, verdant forest lies between County Cavan and County Monaghan. Local folklore claims this is where Cuchulain rested as he single-handedly fought the armies of Maeve as she tried to take over Ulster.

Indeed, many armies fought over this land, beginning with the Gailenga, a tribe inhabiting the glen and guarding the kingdom of Tara from at least the third through sixth centuries. Later armies passed through the glen in the twelfth century (the Normans) and again in the seventeenth century (Cromwell's army).

Dún a Rí hides several ruins beneath the thick forest growth, including the vanished Cabra Village, Fleming Castle (possibly built in 1607) and the Old Military Barracks (circa 1800), which may have been originally built as a stable.

Left: Cabra River
Above: One of the magnificent trees on the green in Dún a Rí.

## Lough Muckno, Castleblayney

One of the largest lakes in County Monaghan, Lough Muckno (or Lake Muckno) is well known for fishing, with stocks of rough fish such as bream and tench, as well as pike. With a depth up to twenty meters, the lake's clear waters offer great opportunities for boating or swimming. Lough Muckno Park sits on the edge of Castleblayney amid 900 acres of woodlands. Many hiking trails offer spectacular views of the lake and surrounding areas.

# River Boyne

Steeped in history and myth, the River Boyne is 70 miles long, running from Trinity Well in County Kildare to the Irish Sea between County Meath and County Louth. The earliest known map of the river is Ptolemy's second century map of Hibernia, wherein he named the river, Bououinda. A thousand years later, Geraldus Cambrensis called it Boandus on his map of Ireland. According to Irish legend, Queen-Goddess Boann created the river, and in its waters, Fionn mac Cumhail (Finn McCool) caught the Salmon of Knowledge.

# Irish Farmland

Though Ireland is changing and modernizing rapidly, the country is still primarily an agrarian nation, with approximately 64% of the land used for agriculture. While walking the lanes or driving anywhere, I often saw cattle and sheep in the fields (and sometimes on the roads).

Both of these pictures were taken near Rosslough, County Louth.

## Charming Back Roads

Hedge walls and curtains of green limit the views from the many lanes and roads criss-crossing Ireland. Like Bilbo Baggins' walking song, the lanes of Ireland invite the traveller ever, ever on, if only to see what's around the bend or just over the hill. The road above winds through the area near Stonestown.

This is the lane past Dad's cottage in Rosslough, perfect for an early morning hike or late night stroll. The light on summer nights in Ireland doesn't fade until after nine. At the top of this lane is a farm, with views of the rolling hills covered in heather. There is also a big dog, silent and watchful.

# Dad's Back Garden

No survey of Ireland's wild places off the beaten track would be complete without mentioning my Dad's back garden. Filled with cedar trees and brambles, the boggy ground made a perfect home for all sorts of wildlife, especially water-loving amphibians. Dad called it the Frog Ranch.

Dad's cottage. You would never guess from the neat front how wild the back can be. Welcome to Ireland: land of many surprises and delights.

# A Quick Pronunciation Guide

Please note that pronunciation differs in different parts of Ireland. Also, many of these names for people and places have several different spellings in English. Irish spelling is quite regular and phonetic, once you know it.

## PEOPLE

| | | |
|---|---|---|
| Benandonner | /ben-an-DON-ner/ | A Scottish giant |
| Clíodhna | /KLEE-na/ | Legendary queen of the Banshees |
| Cuchulain | /ku-HOOL-n/ | Legendary Irish hero |
| Fionn mac Cumhaill | /fin-mak-KOOL/ | Legendary Irish hero (Finn McCool) |
| Laoghaire | /LAY-her-ə/ | Fifth century High King of Ireland |
| Medb | /mayv/ | Legendary Irish warrior queen, (Maeve) |
| Oonagh | /OO-na/ | Finn McCool's wife |
| Ruscaire | /ROO-skah-rə/ | Scottish giant |
| Tuatha dé Danann | TOO-ah-ha day DAA-nən/ | The supernatural people of the goddess, Danu, often associated with powerful Fairies. |

## PLACES

| | | |
|---|---|---|
| An Mhainistir Mhór | /an-VAN-ish-ter-vor/ | Mellifont Abbey (the big abbey) |
| Boirrean | /bur-ren/ | Burren (the rocky place) |
| Brú na Bóinne | /BRU-na--BON-ye/ | Newgrange and area (the mansion of the Boyne) |
| Cahir | /ker/ | Cahir Castle, on the River Suir |
| Carrick á rede | /KER-ik-ah-reed-ə/ | An island off the north coast of Ireland (rock in the road) |
| Cnoc na Teamreach | /krok-na-TE-wra/ | An sacred hill in the Boyne Valley (Hill of Tara) |
| Carraig Machaire Rois | /KER-ik-ma-her-ə-raash/ | Carrickmacross (rock of the wooded plain) |
| Donaghmoyne | /DO-na-moin/ | A parish near Carrickmacross |
| Drogheda | /DRO-he-da/ | A port town on the East Coast of Ireland |
| Dún a Rí | /DUN-ah-ree/ | Forest Park - Co. Cavan & Co. Monaghan (fort of the king) |
| Lisnagunnion | /LIZ-na-GOON-yun/ | A parish near Carrickmacross |
| Louth | /Laoh/ | A small county in the Republic of Ireland |
| Machaire Rois | /MAH-her-raash/ | Magheross Church and Graveyard (wooded plain) |
| Monaghan | /MON-ə-han/ | City and County in the Republic of Ireland |
| Rosslough | /RAAS-loH/ | A township near Carrickmacross (lake of the woods) |
| Taafe Castle | /TAAF/ | A fortified house in Carlingford |
| Thosel Gate | /TOS-el-gayt/ | The old town gate in Carlingford |
| Táin Bó Cúilnge | /TOYN-bo-kul-nyə/ | The great Irish epic- *The Cattle Raid of Cooley*. |

Made in the USA
Middletown, DE
28 May 2022